Old EGREMONT
by
E. Alan Read

This terrace is called Cringlethwaite, meaning 'clearing in the woodland at the bend in the river', and was built in 1895 on the rising ground above Woodbank house. The cost of this sizeable mansion was one of the factors that led to the bankruptcy of its builder, Samuel Sherwen. A very successful wholesale grocer and provision merchant in Whitehaven, he got into unfamiliar territory and overstretched himself when he speculated in coal mining.

© E. Alan Read 2002
First published in
the United Kingdom, 2002,
by Stenlake Publishing
Telephone / Fax: 01290 551122

ISBN 1 84033 206 9

THE PUBLISHERS REGRET THAT
THEY CANNOT SUPPLY COPIES
OF ANY PICTURES FEATURED
IN THIS BOOK.

ACKNOWLEDGEMENT

The publishers would like to thank F. W. Shuttleworth for permission to use the photographs on pages 23 and 26. All other photographs are from the E. A. Read Collection.

By the same author:

Discovering Egremont
1000 Years of Egremont

These books are not available from Stenlake Publishing, but copies can be ordered by visiting
www.egremontcumbriabooks.com

Left: Gordon 'Dodger' Pattinson was a well-loved Egremont character. In his youth he was a keen soccer player (it was on the football pitch that he got his nickname), playing for the then popular Cleator Moor Celtic team. He was also passionately fond of fox-hunting, and would walk many miles over some of England's roughest terrain following the hounds. A mineworker at Florence and Ullcoats mines, he greatly looked forward to his sport each weekend which provided the freedom of the fells and the joy of being in the fresh air. He was an active participant at the annual Crab Fair, where he could be seen gurning, pipe smoking and singing hunting songs to the delight of spectators. Dodger died shortly after Crab Fair day in 1988, aged 86. His legacy lives on in the skilfully carved walking sticks and shepherds' crooks that he made. This photograph shows him enjoying a yard of ale in the bar of the Fox & Hounds after a hunt.

Right: Alfred Gardiner, clogger, worked alongside his son Jack in the small workshop seen behind him here in the lee of the Parish Church, whilst his wife attended to her small footwear shop at 9 Market Place. His skills in the making and repairing of iron-caulkered wooden clogs were in constant demand. No other footwear was as tough or gave greater protection to the feet than the ubiquitous clog, which was standard footwear among iron ore miners. Alf passed away in 1956 having spent a lifetime serving the mining community of Egremont. The cottages known as Dent View adjacent to his workshop no longer stand.

INTRODUCTION

Egremont is an ancient market town whose origins date back to before the first millennium. In historical sources, before spellings became standardised, its name appears in many different ways including Agremond, Egremond, Egrement, Eggermeth and Eggermouth. The name is essentially self-explanatory and means 'the place at the mouth of the River Egger'. This small river, now named the Ehen, flows from Broadwater, the ancient name for Ennerdale Water, a lake some four miles east by north of today's town. In prehistoric days it is said that the river entered the sea at Egremont, the valley between Sellafield and Eggermouth being a tidal estuary at that time.

The area has connections with the Sesuntii, an ancient section of the Brigante tribe which roamed the whole of the northern domains of England for many centuries. It is said that they used Castle Hill as a natural fortress and stronghold some 2,000 years ago, its prominent position above the valley making it ideal for such a purpose.

In AD 79 there were systematic incursions by the Roman general Julius Agricola during his victorious march from Lancaster to Carlisle. It was the Romans who laid out roads, or 'high streets' as they called them, including one along the line of what is now Egremont's Main Street. This was built to facilitate travel between the safe anchorage of Ravenglass and their forts at Moresby and Papcastle. The Roman road was some fifteen feet in width and constructed of cobbles and freestone. It met with the road leading from St Bega, now St Bees, and a 'cross', most probably a stoup of sandstone, was erected at the junction.

After the departure of the Romans, the native Britons of the area had to contend with the incursions of Angles, Jutes and Saxons. Many changes took place over the intervening centuries: there was integration between these different groups, the language changed, beliefs altered and the populace became more cosmopolitan. Place names ending in the word 'ton' – Coulderton, Carleton, Wilton, Irton, Santon etc. – are Anglian in origin, while part of two Saxon burial crosses can still be seen in the old churchyard of St Bridget's (Low Church) near Beckermet.

Next came the Vikings, although whether this was by design or accident will never be known for certain; there are no records other than the fact that Castle Hill was the site of a Danish fortification. It is known that in good weather conditions the Danes could see the Egremont area from their settlements on the Isle of Man, and having crossed the sea they proceeded to settle in this nearby new land. Many words in our everyday language are legacies of their heritage, including fell, dyke, garth, thwaite and numerous others. Place-names ending in the Danish word 'by' are to be found around the area as in Asby, Moresby, Allerby, Arkleby and Allonby.

The actual township of Egremont can be traced back to the time of the Normans, for it was they who further developed Castle Hill, building a type of fortification known as a motte and bailey. The bailey or outer wall of this castle would have been constructed of timber, plentiful supplies of which could be found in the vast area known as the Copland Forest. This was a huge area of woodland stretching from beyond Moresby in the north to the river Duddon in the south, from the foothills of the encircling mountains of the east and almost to the sea in the west. But despite their castle the Normans – as others had before them – found subjugating the Northern people to be a very protracted affair.

Frequent forays upon their stockade fortification on Castle Hill prompted the constantly harried invaders to begin the long and laborious task of building a more permanent structure in sandstone. To their credit this was accomplished, despite many long and bloody battles with both the native population and the Scots, who laid claim to the area as part of the Kingdom of Strathclyde. It took almost 130 years to complete the castle. However, at no time after it was completed was it ever breached, the building and its position proving to be impregnable to every adversary other than nature. The sad ruins of today are proof that no man-made structure can withstand the ravages of time.

Down the ages many powerful family names have been recorded in the castle's history, including le Meschine, Fitzduncan, de Multon, de Lucy, Percy, Fitzwalter, Seymour, Wyndham and Leconfield. Now what remains is in the ownership of Lord Egremont of Petworth House, Sussex. The castle ceased to be occupied as a residence several centuries ago due to the fact that no male heirs were born to anyone other than the infamous Fitzduncan. His son, said to have been the only male child ever born in Egremont Castle, died in tragic circumstances when still a youngster. His memory lives on in Samuel Rogers' poem *The Boy of Egremont*. As a result of his lineage (made complicated by intermarriage and inheritance) this young man had important connections and had he lived would have had greater claims to the throne than the man who was crowned King Henry II.

Through perseverance, the Normans and their heirs gradually won over the local populace, who by the example of their masters learned to build homesteads of river cobbles that were far superior to their former hovels of wattle and clay. These new buildings had permanency, and under the auspices of their overlords the population living around the perimeter of the castle walls grew year by year until a small town was formed. This town was jointly dependent upon the castle residents and the success of the agriculture of the fertile valley and lands towards the coast.

The town was granted its own market charter by King Henry III *c.*1267. This gave it the right in perpetuity to hold a weekly market, and an annual three-day fair. The market still prospers though it is not of the same stature as the original. The fair – now world-renowned as the Crab Fair – grows in popularity annually and is looked forward to with enthusiasm.

Egremont was once the chosen seat of powerful lords and was more recently well known as a source of high grade haematite ore. It grew affluent from industrialism and had a variety of excellent shops. Modern-day Egremont is known for its genial inhabitants, but the town is gradually being downgraded to somewhere of 'no importance' due to a serious lack of inward investment. With its many attributes it could and should be a magnet for tourism, the best hope of tomorrow's wealth.

The parish church of St Mary and St Michael has a magnificent peal of eight bells weighing a total of 2 tons 13 cwt. 21 lb. These were presented to the church in 1902 by Lord Leconfield, owner of the castles both at Egremont and Cockermouth. For many years the church had one of the finest teams of bell-ringers in the county. They won many competitions and are seen here having rung a peal of bob major consisting of 5,008 changes in three hours eight minutes on 7 May 1921 under their conductor William T. Holmes.

This view of Market Place looking north towards the Main Street dates from 1926. The town's principal feature, a broad expanse of uninterrupted roadway, is evident in this photograph, which includes the avenue of trees planted in 1888. The lack of traffic could be attributed to Egremont being in a state of deep depression due to the national coal strike of 1926 (which also affected the local iron ore mines) – or it could just be a quiet Sunday morning in late spring. The second building on the left was the Mechanics Institute, a seat of learning with a huge library, all the latest newspapers and periodicals, plus a billiard room where men could indulge in a few minutes sport with their pals. This unfortunately closed in the mid-1920s due to lack of support, after which the building was demolished and the National Westminster Bank erected on the site. The peacefulness of the scene is almost unbelievable when compared with the bustle and traffic of today.

An 1895 photograph looking from Market Place to South Street. On the left is one of the town's old inns, the Horse & Groom, formerly owned by Dalzells of the Harrington and Parton Brewery. A date-stone above the door at the rear of the property carries the date 1688, while a similar stone at the front is dated 1672. The building next door was a branch of the Whitehaven Joint Stock Bank, and the last shop on the left was occupied by the draper Dobbin. South Street lies beyond. At one time there were over 40 different trades being carried out in small premises in this street, the oldest of which bore a date-stone of 1570. This ancient thoroughfare was needlessly demolished, along with North Road, in the 1960s. The two streets characterised Egremont's long history, having been built with stone quarried from the disused castle and its surrounding walls. Prior to demolition the narrow roadway had been carefully negotiated by extraordinary wide loads on their way to the complex at Sellafield during its construction over a ten year period from 1950 to 1960, with over 3,000 vehicles per day passing along it at the height of the work.

This peaceful scene from the early twentieth century shows the Calvary steps (so-named because John Wesley preached from them on his tour of Britain) with the fish stone (a stone once used by fishmongers for the sale of locally-caught fish) being put to good use as a seat. The delivery lad (from William Clarke's grocery store, on the right) has time to stop for a chat with the old 'uns, while the young lady looks to be out shopping. The blinds at Gainor's the butcher are drawn and the sun shade is out at Joe Suddart's Glasgow & Manchester Warehouse (converted from the old Horse & Groom building). Beyond, the blinds are also drawn at Dobbin's the draper, and in South Street the sun shade shields the window of the former home of Francis Smith, tailor. He is said to be buried in the churchyard immediately behind the property, over the wall of the back yard. It must have been a bright sunny day or maybe half day closing on a Wednesday.

A forerunner of today's mean machines, this photograph shows a once very popular AJS motorcycle of the late 1920s. Note in particular the klaxon horn and the hub brake on the front wheel. The number plate, with its RM prefix, denotes registration in Cumberland. This great advance in transport saved its owner Thomas Mandell (of North Road) many long miles of walking to and from the Ullcoats iron ore mine where he worked as a joiner. The man sitting on the bike, Charlie Wilson, is only acting the part whilst Thomas gets a photo of his new machine in 1928. Charlie's footwear is of interest being typical of the period – duck-neb clogs with leather uppers and iron caulkered wooden soles. Substantial, no-nonsense clogs like these were warm and comfortable and hence very popular.

The well-fed youngster on the left of this 1920s photograph is the author, Ernest Alan Read. Kneeling to attend to the necessary repairs to the 'shakabone' is his elder brother William Irving, subsequently a mechanic with Cumberland Motor Services. On 24 May 1940, serving in the Royal Army Ordnance Corps in Belgium, he became Thornhill's first casualty of the Second World War. The lad proudly holding their prized possession is George Matthews, who served with the RAF in Bomber Command. After the aircraft on which he was a crew member was shot down he was held for a considerable time as a prisoner of war in the notorious Stalag Luft III camp in Poland. He now lives in the Wolverhampton area. But the photograph was taken during the halcyon days of childhood, every one bringing a new adventure. Mend and make do was trendy – some pram wheels, an old bike frame (no saddle, but at least it had a bell), a bit of determined ingenuity – and three lads were off into a make-believe world.

Egremont of the past saw many examples of this particular mode of conveyance, especially on market days. Tom Wood (driving) and Ned Swainson (the father of Tom's wife, Polly) have arrived in town in style. Gone are the normal workaday togs of the out-of-town farmer; instead both men look as though they mean business.

This 1946 photograph shows Alan Read, cartwright, of W. W. Gardiner's Vale View Joinery Works. The skilled trades of cartwright and wheelwright gradually disappeared as horse-power diminished and tractors found favour on almost all local farms from the 1930s onwards. A block cart, like the one seen here, was able to safely carry loads of between one and one and a half tons on 4' 6" wooden wheels, the whole lot being pulled by a single powerful cart horse. This most versatile of vehicles was built from local timber (oak, ash, elm and larch), and required the combined skills of the cartwright and blacksmith in its construction. In the background is a stack of wooden potato seed boxes, another item that has disappeared from the modern-day farm. Fifty years ago these were made in great quantities, keeping young apprentices busy by the hour.

Bridge End garage was built on part of the site of one of the town's four tanneries. This one was often referred to as Mossop's tannery, although it was actually built in 1750 on reclaimed riverside land by William Benson, an entrepreneurial member of an old-established Egremont family. At one point the garage premises belonged to the Egremont Motor Bus Company. When this ceased trading, they were taken over by Ben Moffat who built up a profitable business which diversified when he became interested in the then newfangled wireless. Ben was agent for the well-known Cossor brand, which he sold and repaired. In this photograph Ben Moffat, with arms folded, chats to the unknown owner of an expensive-looking car, probably a Humber Classic of the 1930s. Note the petrol pump: the handle above the plinth was pushed backwards and forwards to deliver half a gallon of fuel at a time. In 1946 Ben vacated the premises and Henry Graham, demobbed from his wartime services, took over. Through his enterprise and hard work he became a very successful motor engineer, moving from this site into custom-built premises in 1962. The old garage was demolished shortly afterwards.

In 1861 a horse-drawn pump capable of pumping in excess of 100 gallons per minute under the capable hands of six men was bought by public subscription. This motorised version (which was housed in a wooden shed behind the Market Hall) was concocted from a Model T Ford whose saloon body was replaced with the pump from the original horse-drawn fire engine. Thus innovation and ingenuity provided Egremont with its first motor-driven fire fighting appliance, dating from about 1920.

These eighteen lusty lads of E Company 5th Battalion Border Regiment were photographed during the early part of the Great War of 1914–1918 during training before being sent into combat. Though their individual names are unknown, a reader may recognise one or more as being among their forebears. The war memorial in Market Place bears all of the names of those local personnel who served and made the supreme sacrifice during both the First and Second World Wars, and helps to bring the faces in this photograph vividly into focus. It is only right and fitting that these men should be remembered; several among their rank died so that we could live in peace.

The 10th Cumberland (Egremont) Rifle Volunteers were formed in 1862 and in 1864 established their own band under the direction of Honorary Major Thomas Harrison. In 1900 they became part of the newly formed 1st Volunteer Battalion of the Border Regiment M Company under Captain James E. Syme of Rosewell Garth, Bookwell. James Syme was well-known and respected within veterinary circles both in and around Egremont and the Isle of Man where he also owned property. At the outbreak of the First World War the men of the 1st Volunteer Battalion became part of the 5th Battalion Border Regiment Territorial Force. Many of their names are recorded on the war memorial in Market Place. This picture was taken in 1864 outside Gillfoot Mansion, the home of Thomas Hartley Esq.

At the start of the First World War those men who had played in the E Company band of the 5th Battalion Border Regiment were called to the colours, and it was left to those who stayed behind to work in the iron ore mines and quarries to maintain the spirit of the well-known band. From this nucleus Egremont Town Band grew and still survives today. The men pictured here are among the forefathers of those who give so much pleasure now – they make no charge for their services and are entirely dependent on the general public for financial support. This photograph was taken in the grounds of the castle by W. J. Meckin of 47 Main Street, a respected member of the community and very competent photographer of the period. Many of his postcards can now be found in the hands of private collectors and are eagerly sought after.

The town band proudly fronts the Children's Gala of 1923 while milling crowds throng the Main Street and Market Place to watch the huge parade. It is mid-July, fine but not sunny (at least there are no shadows to verify sunshine), but the town is shining on this celebratory occasion. I would have been two years old at the time and may have been in the crowd with my parents. The trees in the picture were planted to form an avenue in 1888. When electric street lighting was proposed in 1922 the whole street was declared to be an area of beauty that should not be despoiled by unsightly lamp standards!

Most young girls love dressing up, though to win first prize at a gala and be crowned Fairy Queen must have made for the most thrilling day of a youngster's life. All the children in this 1923 photograph are beautifully attired in painstakingly made costumes, complete with tiaras and magic wands. These youngsters are probably now great grandmas to children of a similar age, and will perhaps tell them stories of that great era.

The crowd of onlookers surges forward for a better view of the superbly decorated dray as the Fairy Queen and her entourage pass the new police station, from which the officers' wives have a great vantage point. Surely the man leading the horse is one of the Winters family? The onlookers are as excited as the children on the float – there is nothing an Egremothian likes better than a good parade. Salford Terrace, behind the telegraph pole, was built in 1900. The little shop to its left was a butcher's under the ownership of Samuel West when this photograph was taken; Samuel later moved to 48 Main Street. Note the sign at the top left-hand corner of the premises behind the Fairy Queen float. It advertises BSA Cycles and indicates that the shop was owned at the time by Harry Lewthwaite (see also page 44).

CHILDRENS GALA EGREMONT JULY 18th 1923

The bloody conflict of the First World War lingered in people's minds for a long time afterwards, and on Gala Day peace was celebrated and the fallen of the war remembered. Here a Union flag is being held aloft, while youngsters dressed in sailors' outfits carry an anchor surrounded by a wreath in tribute to those who perished on Naval duties. The decorated float depicts all aspects of the military services, represented by children who were probably born after the cessation of hostilities, but who were keen to show their loyalty to a father or grandfather who had seen duty in the forces.

Throughout its history Egremont has always suffered periods of boom and recession due to its traditional dependence on a single dominant source of income. This was once agriculture, then iron ore mining, whilst nowadays the complex at Sellafield provides the majority of local jobs. However, during periods of privation or difficulty, the people of Egremont have always shown a strong community spirit. In June 1922 a memorial to the town's war dead was unveiled in front of one of the largest crowds ever to assemble in the Market Place and Main Street, with the Border Regiment standing guard alongside. An appeal had raised over £5,000 for the construction of the monument, which features a bronze figure of a soldier attired in the uniform of the time standing on a granite plinth. Virtually the whole town was present at the event, and the first floor windows of the businesses adjacent to the memorial were filled with onlookers. These businesses included Isaac W. Nicholson, cabinetmaker; Stout's Garage; the Red Lion Hotel; Calvert Thompson, milliner; Charles Birbeck, outfitter; the Blue Bell Inn; Jack Graham, stationer; Mary Abbott, fruiterer; Alf Gardiner, clogger; and Joseph Suddart's Glasgow & Manchester Warehouse.

Local support for the Empire is clearly illustrated by this smartly decorated horse-drawn float. A troop of scouts act as an escort, followed by children in traditional dress representative of all parts of the Empire. The richness of the trappings and the pride of taking part is visible everywhere. Egremont had recently passed through the hell of wartime, losing many sons in the course of service to the nation. The town's residents were now showing their determination to ensure a new generation of children grew up with a touch of magic and wonder in their lives.

The houses on the right were built of local rose-coloured sandstone in the mid-nineteenth century by the Mossop family, who also came to own the tanyard opposite the larger house with the steps and iron handrail. That house was built by William Benson, who was also responsible for the construction of the tanyard on the river's edge opposite, although he died shortly after the business began to operate. The road in front of the houses was the main route into town using the old 'Burras Brigge' (Borough Bridge). It was here that the road from Beckermet via Lowmill joined with routes from Carlton, Haile and Wilton. Until 1565 the River Ehen was crossed by ford at this point; the bridge that replaced it was superseded by a more modern structure in 1822. Even with the huge volume of traffic using the road today, this still gives good service. Following on from Bridge End into the narrows of Vale View, the building in the left foreground (which was probably once part of the tanyard complex) was Alex Thompson's workshop. The tall sandstone building behind this was a fulling mill used for the pounding of flax fibres. Next was Vale View Joinery Works, originally a sailcloth mill. The small row of terraced cottages beyond were built in 1878 on the very edge of the river. The lord of the manor is said to have agreed to the site being used in order to prevent further erosion of the river bank at this point and to alleviate the risk of flood damage to Bridge End properties. The kitchens belonging to these cottages are built on girders cantilevered over the river. The small single-storey cottage at the top of this terrace was the toll bar cottage, built in 1856. Anyone entering the town to trade, or travelling with a conveyance or animal, was obliged to pay a toll. This was imposed to help maintain the town's roads.

Iron ore mining played a major part in the development of Egremont, and today the only working iron ore mine in the whole of Europe – the Florence No. 2 mine – stands on the town's doorstep. Much of the land that Egremont is built on is honeycombed with a labyrinth of mine workings that lie at varying depths below the surface. The central and northern parts of the town, and the areas lying to its north and east, contained over 25 mines, all of which are now filled with water, which prevents major subsidence. Winscales No. 1 mine, illustrated here, was part of the Beckermet Mining Company group and once employed many hundreds of men above and below ground. At the onset of the First World War a new shaft was sunk and a railway link was planned to connect it with the old No. 1 mine, thereby facilitating the conveyance of ore to the smelters at Workington. However, way-leave over the many crossing points proved to be rather expensive and to get round this a drift was driven between the two mines and the ore transported underground.

Miners worked by candlelight for the first few years of operation at Winscales mine before carbide lamps were introduced. All the drilling was originally carried out laboriously by hand, using a four or six pound hammer to hammer the long drills into the rock-face. Gunpowder was then placed in the holes and ignited by a system of fuse wires; the resulting explosion blasted out the rock. Many miners lost their lives in those workings.

Pit top and shaft workers smile broadly while the pit cage awaits the signal to ride the shaft for an examination. *Left to right:* David McGivern, Harry Ivinson, unknown, Derek Morrison, unknown.

Haile Moor, the third mine in the Beckermet group, was sunk during the years of the Second World War with the help of government money. Although the ore obtained was at a very modest depth below the surface – about 130 fathoms – the mine proved to be an uneconomic venture and had a relatively short life. It was almost a mile from No. 1 shaft and had to have an aerial ropeway constructed to carry the small amount of ore obtained over the surrounding countryside. From No. 1 shaft it was transported by rail to the ironworks at Workington over fifteen miles to the north. This picture shows the winding gear and buildings housing the aerial ropeway machinery. Some of the structures are still to be seen above the ancient village of Haile, although the mine closed in 1975 when the subsidies ran out.

Many tasks, some of major proportions, had to be undertaken by the top hands at the numerous iron ore mines in the area. The removal of the huge boiler pictured here at one of the Florence mines was no mean feat. Having served its purpose of supplying copious quantities of steam to the ever-hungry headgear (as well as providing heating for the pit showers etc.), it was in need of replacement and this is part of the small team to whom the job was entrusted. Those featured are, left to right: unknown, Oliver Simpson, William Tyson, Benny Bainbridge. The photograph has the following hand-written message on the back: 'First hard work ever done by Pa at work – removal of a boiler. 1954'!

This historic 1907 photograph was taken outside the Methodist Church in Chapel Street; the prominently displayed notice reads: PLEASE HELP WIVES AND CHILDREN OF MINERS ON STRIKE AT ULLCOATS FOR ONE POUND A FORTNIGHT. The strike lasted for 13 weeks and the miners, through desperation for the well-being of their families, were ultimately forced to return to work three pence per shift worse off. The 112 children depicted here all look well-dressed and well-nourished, as do the few menfolk in the background, but this was at the beginning of the strike. The Methodist Church not only gave the miners and their families spiritual help, but was also instrumental in distributing soup, which was provided from a soup kitchen behind the town hall on the opposite side of the street and served in the schoolroom adjacent to the church. Days like this are best forgotten, although events such as these left an indelible impression even on the youngest minds.

Like all forms of mining, iron ore mining was a dangerous pursuit and many accidents – both large and small – occurred locally. An efficient ambulance team was an essential part of the mining community, and this group from Beckermet mine won many trophies for their skills. By the time this photograph was taken in 1964 the Beckermet group had become part of British Steel (before that it had been owned by the United Steel Company), and the sixteen men illustrated here took part in competitions throughout the whole of British Steel group of subsidiaries.
Left to right: Sidney Cockbain, Cyril Bell, Harold Rogers, Hedley Rodgers, William Akitt, Douglas Lee, John Bigrigg, William Hoyles, Martin Adams, Benjamin Mitchell, Kenneth Troughton, Jack Johnson, Robert Adair, Harold Jackson, Joseph Burns, Arthur Whiston.

This historic photograph was published as a postcard by William J. Meckin, who operated as a photographer from 47 Main Street at the time of the event pictured. Townhead mine was situated opposite the junction of the Cleator Road and the Clintz Brow Woodend Road. In early March 1913 an accident occurred there which resulted in one man being drowned. The mine had been sunk in 1902 and operated in an area riddled with older mine-workings; over the years these had become flooded and during mining operations in 1913 someone inadvertently broke through into the old workings. Water cascaded into Townhead and the whole mine was soon in trouble, with miners running for their lives. Fortunately good local knowledge of the workings allowed 80 men to be led to an adjacent ventilation shaft where they were able to climb a series of ladders and reach the surface 300 feet above. A roll call was made and three men were found to be missing. It was later discovered that one had drowned when the deepening waters overcame him as he climbed the ladders. Another man, John Cairns, had remembered a borehole in another area of the mine and led his fellow miner James Ward there, where having scaled a steep incline they found themselves sixteen feet above the level of the floodwaters. Their location was eventually identified and food, drinking water and candles were lowered to them through the borehole. Two divers from the dockyards of Barrow-in-Furness were summoned to assist in the rescue, while crowds of relatives, friends and curious onlookers gathered at the shaft head to watch the proceedings. The two men remained incarcerated for five days before being rescued. John Cairns was later awarded the King Edward bronze medal for bravery, while the rescuers were presented with commemorative medallions. Townhead mine belonged to Lord Leconfield and was used to win high-grade haematite ore. It closed in 1914.

The Whitehaven, Cleator and Egremont Railway, an independent railway backed by the Lonsdales, was incorporated in June 1854. It ran from Mirehouse Junction, a mile south of Whitehaven Corkickle, to Moor Row and Egremont, with a branch to Cleator Moor and Frizington. During the first six months of its operation over 60,000 tons of iron ore, coke and coal from local mines was transported by the railway and dividends to shareholders rocketed to 13 per cent. In 1857 a small station (above) was built at Egremont when the decision was made to operate passenger services. These proved to be a huge success, with people coming from all points south of the town to experience this modern, comfortable mode of transport. In 1868 the line was extended southwards to join with the Furness Railway's line at what was then a tiny hamlet named Sellafield; now a name known worldwide. A smart waiting room was added at Sellafield many years later in 1954 when trains were used to transport pupils from outside the area to the first purpose-built comprehensive in Britain, the Wyndham School in Egremont town centre. This photograph (taken on 7 May 1954) is by F. W. Shuttleworth.

When the line which ran through Egremont was extended to join the Furness Railway's line at Sellafield, the Whitehaven, Cleator and Egremont Railway became part of the Furness Railway. Its coaches were painted in a chocolate livery, and to the youngsters who made the trip to the seaside at Seascale they were almost good enough to eat. Scores of wildly excited children lined the platform of Egremont station on Sunday school outings to this very popular venue by the Irish Sea, even though it was only some five miles away. Nonetheless, in those now far-off days it was a world away from their normal life. A paper bag containing an iced bun, a small sponge topped with icing and hundreds and thousands, and an apple or an orange helped to make all their dreams a reality on those much looked-forward to trips. This photograph of Furness Railway 0-6-2T engine No. 112 shows the driver, a Mr Costine, and fireman, Mr Sowerby, both of Moor Row.

This branch was built to transport iron ore direct from the Ullbank mine, just south of Egremont station, although the mine visible in this *c.*1880 picture was the Wyndham Company No. 3 shaft (the capped shaft can be seen close by today's fire station). To the left of the smoking pit chimney are the gasworks which were served by another branch from the station named the Donkey Line. This had a very steep gradient, and now forms part of the line of the bypass. The gasworks were built in 1853 with the issue of 120 shares at £10 each and proved to be an immense boon to the general public. Gas lit the main thoroughfare and also became a means of illumination in almost every home, ousting the era of candlelight and oil lamps, and providing hard-pressed housewives with more light by which to run their houses.

Situated by the gasworks, this was one of a group of bridges that were built in 1868 as part of the infrastructure needed to carry the new rail link to Sellafield via Beckermet over the river Ehen in an area known as the Pinfold. This was an ancient gathering place for animals brought in for safe keeping of a evening after grazing on land east of the river, and its origins dated back to the sixteenth century. Like its counterparts, the bridge was demolished in 1991 to make way for the concrete structures needed to carry the bypass. As youngsters, it was a thrill to climb the sandstone buttress and sit with our backs to the metal bridge when a train passed overhead – the resulting noise and vibration was better than riding on Taylor's funfair which visited the Beck Green every Crab Fair week – and of course it was free. The climb up the buttress was a challenge in itself to adventurous lads.

A locomotive prepares to convey two tankers of milk from the Milk Marketing Board's Egremont depot on the daily run to Newcastle via Carlisle. Having collected the tank wagons, the engine is about to run forward and then reverse them gently up to the goods brake van (centre), to which they will be coupled. The locomotive was an 0-6-0 tender engine built by the North British Locomotive Company in 1920 for the Furness Railway, who gave it the number 33. After the railway Grouping of 1923 it became the property of the LM&SR and was renumbered 12510. When the railways were nationalised in 1948 the engine was renumbered again, becoming BR 52510. It was the last engine from the former Furness Railway to remain in service, being withdrawn from Carnforth shed in August 1957. The Milk Marketing Board depot, which is obscured behind the bulk of the Rowntree's chocolate crumb factory in this picture, opened in 1946 (chocolate crumb was a cooked mix of milk, sugar and cocoa that was broken into crumbs and subsequently made into a variety of confectionery products). To the left of the loco, Winscales No. 2 Beckermet mine can be seen on the skyline. Gibson's small bulldozer is clearing the ground around the new (built 1953) Rowntree's factory; this concern eventually used almost every gallon of surplus milk collected from a wide area around Egremont – in excess of 4,000 gallons per day. The railway was at first used to transport the chocolate crumb to Rowntree's main depot at York, while in later years it was transported by road. After the 1954 fire in the UKAEA atomic reactor at Windscales (now Sellafield), the Rowntree's factory was temporarily closed because of fears of milk contamination. It shut for good in 1984 and the factory building was destroyed by fire on 19/20 August 1994 when being used for storage by local entrepreneur Tom O'Fee. The MMB shut down its operations in the district in 1983. This photograph (taken on 7 May 1954) is by F. W. Shuttleworth.

This photograph of a class at the Central Infants School in Egremont was taken between 1904 and 1920. Unfortunately no names are given on the reverse and those who might recall them are few and far between, with eyesight too dim to recognise yesterday's children.

Pupils at Bookwell School photographed in 1930.
Back row: Jack Dixon, T. Long, Henry Kirkby, John Beattie, John Rickerby, Ken Newby, Ken Todhunter, Ken Gilmour.
Middle row: Jim Lewthwaite, Alan Mossop, Harold Watson, Stan Kelly, Bill Hocking, Jim Dixon, Lambert Tyson, Jim Brereton, G. Pattinson, N. McNight, Tommy Taylor.
Front row: B. Wilkinson, Gordon Strickland, Harold Pattinson, Harry Devlin, Jack Tonkin, William Clarke, unknown, Billy Maudie, Puck Howell, John Matterson, Dick Jeffery.

Pupils at Bookwell School photographed in 1927.
Back row: Edward Graham, Eric Ferguson, Kit Horn, Alan Turner, Robert Farragher, J. Matterson, Tommy Malkinson, J. Rooney.
Third row: J. Benn, Gordon Bone, Jim Pullin, T. Bruce, Leslie Bowness, Walter Nichol, John Wise, Eddie Jackman.
Second row: C. Sewell, T. Carlisle, Harry Harrison, L. Kirkbride, Robert Gatenby, W. Duncan, Harry Long, George Wilson, R. Carney.
Front row: Chris Davidson, John Howard, Walter Rosewarne, Graham Eilbeck, W. Walker, William Cook, Billy Tomlinson, John Ferguson, Norman Strickland.

Members of the Egremont Bowling and Tennis Club photographed in 1910 on the steps of the original pavilion, which was opened in 1881 by Jonas Lindow of Ingwell. This small pavilion contained a gymnasium and locker rooms; other facilities belonging to the club included four lawn tennis courts and a bowling green large enough to accommodate six sets of players. There was also space for croquet and quoits, and during times of hard frost the greens used for these could be flooded and became an almost perfect ice-rink. Many enthusiastic folk took full advantage of the various facilities offered by the club over a period of many years, but sadly it folded in the late 1950s due to lack of interest. The land reverted to fields and an important recreational asset was lost. The youngster in the front row is Benson Douglas (later proprietor of the garage in Main Street), seen with his father.

The small hamlet of Low Mill included this terrace, known as the Long Row and situated slightly to the south of the rest of the community. Its small two-up, two-down cottages were occupied by families employed in the manufacture of ropes, sailcloth yarn, shoddy and woollen cloth. There was a small group of water-driven mills within the hamlet, all of which were associated with the larger mills found around the town of Egremont. These larger mills were contracted to supply materials to the shipyards of Whitehaven and Parton. Most of the raw material used by the mills in Egremont and Low Mill was obtained from the versatile flax plant. After harvesting this was steeped in water until it became soft enough to be put through the fulling machine. This separated the useful fibres from the rest of the plant. The families who lived and worked at Low Mill had few facilities. The cottages had no rear entrances (the ultimate reason for their demolition) and almost all had no proper sanitation. A small well provided drinking water whilst all other water was obtained by bucket from the river. Children from the hamlet – said at one time to have numbered more than fifty – were divided between the schools at Beckermet and Egremont. For those attending either of these schools this meant a walk of over three miles there and back each day. The memorial house at Low Mill still stands and has an engraved memorial embedded in the gable end to commemorate those from this small hamlet who gave their lives in the First World War.

During the last three centuries, Cumberland and Westmorland style wrestling was the most popular activity in the annual sporting calendar in the northern counties. The Crab Fair saw its fair share of this well-loved sport being practised, mainly by young men wishing to promote their strength and prowess in the arena, almost like gladiators of bygone ages. Many world championship matches have been settled at the September fair in Egremont. A very popular aside to the actual wrestling was the parade before the matches began. This provided the Queen of the Fair with the opportunity of viewing the contestants at close quarters without being thought forward or offensive, and without the fear of any disparaging remarks being passed by those being ogled! The costumes invariably included velvet trunks which were beautifully embroidered with appropriate motifs by sweethearts or wives of the participants. These were worn over long johns and often accompanied by similarly decorated vests. The man on the right of this picture, standing beside the young lady judging the event, was Peter Kelly, general manager of the Co-op. Peter was one of the most popular MCs at the Crab Fair. The Baybarrow field used for the fair's sporting events is undoubtedly one of the best grounds available, with a view that takes in a major portion of the Western Fells. On a fine September day this view is absolutely stunning.

This picture was taken on Bleach Green in the early 1920s and shows a line-up of Egremont tradesmen (mainly from the Co-op), gathered for a charity football match. What the charity was, or how much the match raised is lost in the mists of time. It's not even clear whether soccer or rugby was being played, and a careful look at some of those who apparently took part suggests that it would have been a hilarious match. A few of the names (left to right) of the participants are known:

Front row: unknown; Sep Harrison, Co-op butcher; Peter Kelly, Co-op draper; Wm. Wyn Eilbeck, shopkeeper; James Blendall, Co-op butcher; unknown; T. Burns, landlord Ship Inn and late manager of the Empire Cinema; unknown.

Back row: unknown; unknown; unknown; James Mitchell, cab proprietor; unknown; Ernest Beatson, Co-op butcher; unknown; James Holliday, landlord King's Arms; Tom Simpson, Co-op drapery manager; William Mawson, joiner; Adam Tyson; Edward Dickinson, manager of Kitty Roberts' grocery; Marshall Wood, schoolmaster (Rookwell); Justus Thomas, general manager of the Co-op.

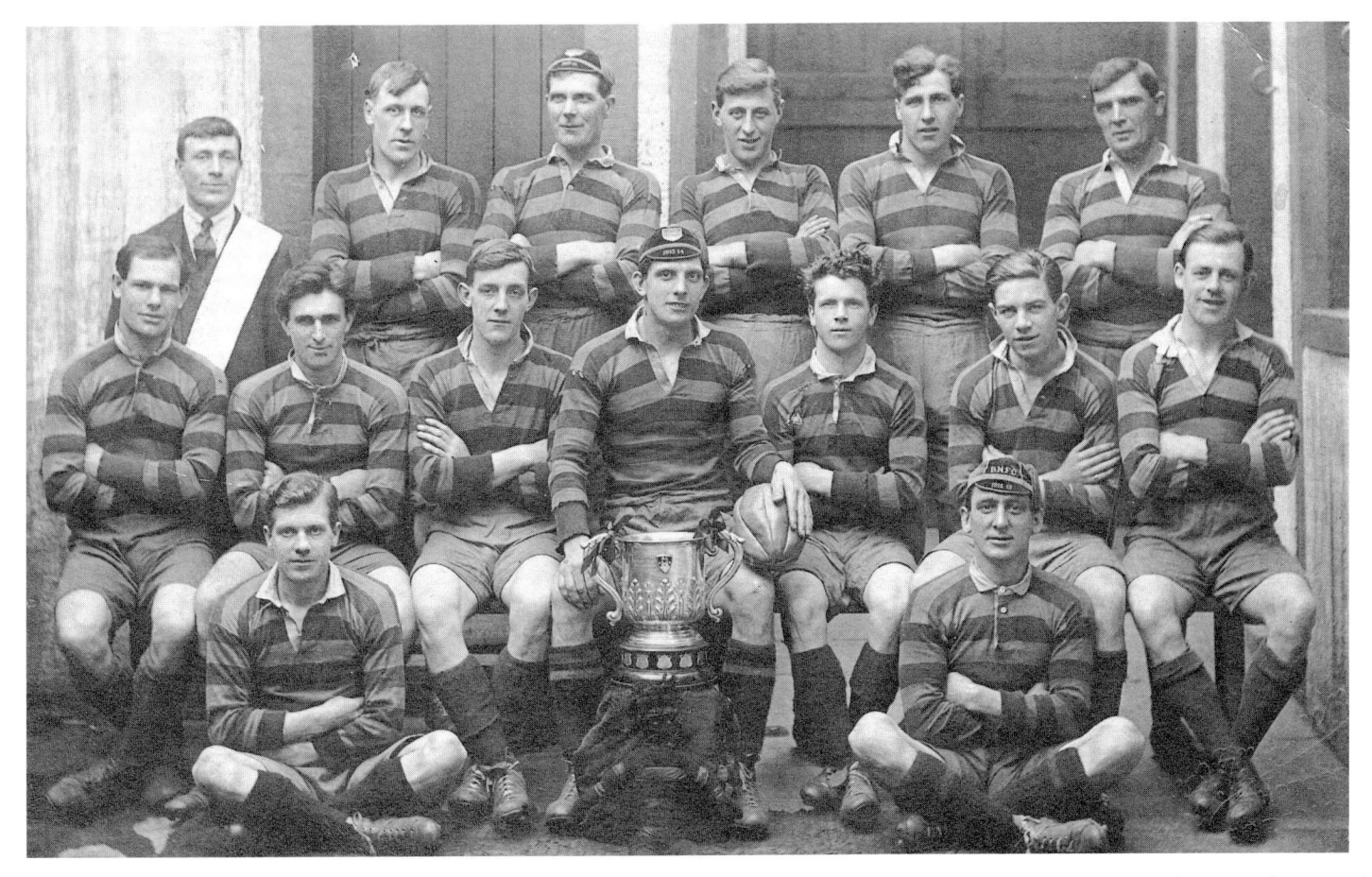

Sport has always played an important part in the lives of Egremothians, and Rugby, both Union and League, has maintained its popularity with both adults and youngsters over the years. The group shown here should stir the memories of many townsfolk, as many of today's players are related to these early stalwarts. The picture shows the Cumberland Cup winners of what was previously called the Northern Union, a group of teams from the north of England whose name was changed to the Rugby League in 1909.

Back row: unknown, Buller Copeland, Joss Hall, Bill Cowan, unknown, Tom Hall
Middle: unknown, unknown, Charlie Adams, George Hall, unknown, Alf Cowan, unknown
Front: unknown, Marshall Rodgers.

The cap worn by Marshall Rodgers is a Bradford Northern cap belonging to George Hall who is wearing a County cap, as is Joss Hall.

According to legend, the King's Arms has been the scene of many memorable events concerning the history of Egremont, with ghostly apparitions manifesting themselves to certain landlords and members of their staff. It was used as a courthouse in the seventeenth and eighteenth centuries, and convicted felons were led from the inn to Gibbet Holme for execution by hanging or beheading. The inn was also a posting house for the collection of both passengers and mail, with a regular service (three times weekly) on the Ulverston to Whitehaven run. When this photograph was taken c.1924 the landlord was Thomas Fawcett.

Whoever named this tiny cobbled court Providence Place surely had a peculiar sense of humour. There was hardly room to swing a cat in these tiny cottages, which had no rear entrances and for most of their lifetime no sanitation or running water. The death rate of children born into cottages like these – and there were a good number in the town – meant that as many as one in three perished before they reached five years of age. Despite the unhealthy conditions, large families were often the norm, and in the late nineteenth century cholera and smallpox were rife in the overcrowded dwellings. Despite the privations, parents strove to ensure their offspring grew up in a clean environment, and there are still people alive today who have happy memories of childhoods spent in courts similar to Providence Place. Sandwith's Court and Williamson's Lane (or Young's Terrace as it was latterly known) were both situated off Church Street. Blue Bell Lane, Chamber's Court and Dent View were off Market Place, while Lucas Court, Swan Lane, Hodgson's Court, Beck Place, Nicholson's Court, Bank Lane and Hartley's Court are among those that were situated off Main Street.

This aerial photograph of 1947 is of great interest as in addition to the castle it shows the south end of the town before its unwarranted decimation during the 1960s by the then local authority, Ennerdale Rural District Council. Most of South Street, including Hatter's Lane, Providence Place, and part of Tyson's Lane were destroyed during the demolition programme, as well as the whole of Croft Terrace and most of Church Street including Sandwith's Court and Young's Terrace. Other equally interesting areas disappeared around the same time. The town's oldest farm can be seen at the extreme right of the picture at the foot of the area known as the Pleasance. This was Pits Farm, the site of the original saw pit where most of the timbers used in the building of the castle would have been sawn.

Church Street was a street of great variety, which included along its length one or two large town houses and a Methodist Chapel (used at a later date as a blacksmith's shop by Henry Herd & Son). There were two public houses: the Forrester's Arms and the Robin Hood, and two courts of tiny cottages branched off the street. A church has stood on the same site in Church Street since c.1130, but has been rebuilt three times and altered on numerous occasions. The present-day St Mary's & St Michael's was built between 1881 and 1883 and for quite a number of yards its old graveyard comes to the road edge. In addition to these more prominent features, there were sixty cottages built of small sandstone blocks or cobbles presenting a well-ordered and congenial thoroughfare. The only business now in Church Street is Hartley's ice cream shop and factory, which has sated children's appetites for many years. Take particular note of the women's pinnies and the little girl's dress, all of which are whiter than white although there were no washing machines in those days – just honest-to-goodness scrubbing after a boil with white Windsor or carbolic soap and the addition of a little 'dolly blue'.

Officially called Croft Terrace but known by many of its older residents as Rook Field, this cul-de-sac of well-constructed cottages was built on a field belonging to John Rook, miller and farmer (who owned and worked Great Mill and Lord's Mill off South Street) in the middle of the nineteenth century. The terrace was a lively place whose residents were always to the fore when there were any celebrations. Here they are about to participate in a sumptuous spread to commemorate VE Day on 8 May 1945. No one could better this small street in providing what they termed a co-operative tea party, and everyone joined in to make it a huge success.

8 South Street, which bore the date 1580 above its door, was destroyed in 1968 under the guise of road widening by Egremont's then local authority. It was a house of legend, said to have had a secret underground passageway leading to the castle forecourt. A former occupant of the house was head forester to the castle lord and is reputed to have had an illicit love affair with his daughter, meeting her secretly within the dark confines of the passage. The legend does not stop there, for apparently they stole away into the night and though hunted far and wide were never seen again. No. 8 was one of a small group of houses which had written legal rights to dig for peat on Black Moss to the east of the town. The stone above the door has the letters 'J. P.' to the left of the date and the letter 'M.' to its right. J. P. probably stands for John Ponsonby, who built and owned properties in Egremont. The occupant of the house prior to its demolition, Phillip Clucas, was a barber by trade and also the town's first licensed bookmaker.

37

The skill and ingenuity of the designers and builders of this impressive float are immediately apparent. It formed part of the Festival of Britain celebrations in 1951, and was rather ahead of its time regarding its complement. A ship crewed by WRENS would have been unheard of in those days, but how could Egremont have a carnival without some of its female residents participating? Their sailor suit outfits caused many oohs and aahs as the splendid vessel floated down the street.

The Thornhill Gaybirds were a very popular group of amateur performers who were in great demand at many local venues. They travelled widely during the 1960s, and their services helped to garner much-needed funds for pensioner groups and church funds. One of their regular spots was at Irton Hall, where they entertained the handicapped youngsters. Mary Dixon accompanied the versatile group on the piano, with Elvina Quayle (Jenkinson) in charge of choreography. John Farren and Joyce Shepherd gave invaluable service in charge of props and wardrobe duties. The guest comedian Norman Hunter entertained in his own inimitable manner. Most of the cast of twelve are still to be found actively engaged in community life, though time has tended to curtail their more strenuous activities. Those featured are:

Standing: Ruth Sherwen, Ivy Hewitson, Brenda Burton, Pam Oldfield, Betty Farren, Doris Ward, Annie Jeffery, Margaret Telford.

Kneeling: Sylvia Earl, Sheila Mulholland, Eleanor Jagger.

On the night of 16 January 1962 part of Egremont was devastated by a mini tornado. This struck with tremendous force around 11.30 p.m. damaging over fifty homes. The ferocious wind came in from the sea, leaving in its wake a huge amount of debris in a fairly narrow path from Picket How, where the damage began, onwards. The pavilion on Bleach Green was shredded into a thousand pieces and bits of roofing from houses in the vicinity of Bridge End were torn off. The Villas were next in line – a new bungalow being built at the time had sarking felt ripped off in huge strips. The Manse at 3 The Villas (pictured here), home of the Methodist minister, lost 90 per cent of its roof with debris causing damage to Nos. 1 and 2. Homes in Croft Terrace shook with the pressure imposed upon them in those few moments. Many lost batches of slates and timbers and some homes had to be evacuated – it was reminiscent of bombing raids during the war. At Beck Green the prefabricated bungalows shuddered with the impact and one house was torn from its foundations and carried over 30 feet. Other bungalows lost their roofs completely, and pieces of debris were subsequently found half a mile away over the river in Fargy's field. The tornado lasted only a few seconds but left the town trembling with fear. Many theories have been put forward as to its cause. One of the suggestions was that it could have come about as a result of the space programme of the time. A relatively large number of items were being launched into space during this period, and it was proposed that the tornado had been caused by a piece of space debris re-entering the earth's atmosphere. Such an object would have created a considerable vacuum in its wake. Whatever its cause the tornado certainly left its mark on Egremont.

This photograph was taken at the opening of the castle grounds to the public on 19 August 1913. These had just been taken over from Lord Leconfield of Cockermouth Castle by the Urban District Council at a peppercorn rent. Many hours were spent remedying the dereliction of several centuries, and a new perimeter wall was built incorporating an imposing entrance of studded teak doors. This was a celebratory day for Egremont – the ancient ruins of this once powerful edifice were to become an integral part of everyday life instead of being an out of bounds ruin. Having been tastefully laid out with lawns and flower beds, the grounds became an area of outstanding beauty, ideal for a spot of quiet contemplation. In later days a small summerhouse was added.

The building on the right was Egremont's largest tannery. It was built by the Nicholson family, who were previously yeoman farmers and had been residents of the parish from the time of Elizabeth l. The business was established in 1720 and lasted for almost two hundred years, closing in 1911 when owned by the very well-known Downes family. Its products were recognised by the leather industry as being of superb quality. On the extreme left of the picture is the frontage of the original Roman Catholic church of 1907. Of timber and corrugated iron construction, this served the populace extremely well until 1960 when it was demolished and replaced by a superb new structure. The castle gardens, so tastefully laid out with flower beds and lawns, were the pride and joy of the head gardener, Mr Wildig, a man well-named for one of his profession. Woe betide anyone who so much as put a foot on his perfect lawns or plucked one flower from his immaculate spring, summer and autumn displays!

The Co-op in Egremont came about through the efforts of a small group of entrepreneurs who, having read of the spreading movement (which originated in Rochdale), made a decision to establish such a society in an old blacksmith's workshop in Blue Bell Lane. This decision dates back to the year 1859, after which the enterprise grew at a prodigious rate. By 1868 the society had moved to the Main Street where brand spanking new headquarters were built on land previously occupied by four tiny cottages. The land, which was owned by Sir Robert Briscoe, was obtained at a bargain price. The building in the picture still dominates the Main Street, although many alterations have been made over the years. Due to the society's success, additional branches had to be built at nearby Thornhill, Beckermet, Gosforth, East Road, Gully Flats and Smithfield, with property also acquired in Seascale. The movement was of inestimable value to the local population, providing its customers with everything from an ounce of tobacco to a complete house furnishing service. The Co-op was a good employer, paying generous wages to the many staff in their employ, and providing a variety of benefits unheard of in similar workplaces elsewhere. The names on the back of this photograph are as follows, although unfortunately the list is not complete and it is not clear which name belongs to which person: Edward Dickinson, Joseph Cartner, Joseph Marsden, Douglas Mandale, Gerald Griffiths, Arnold Harkness, Joseph Graham, William Benn, Annie Mawson.

42

This photograph was taken in 1965 just prior to the demolition of all of these properties by Ennerdale Rural District Council. The premises on the right with the customer almost at its door belonged to Gino Sisi and was a most popular venue when the small Palace Cinema stood almost opposite, at the entrance to Old Bridge Road. The black and white silent films were accompanied by Jonah Prince on the piano. A trip out to see a film and enjoy fish and chips with an ice cream sundae afterwards at Gino's was a very special treat that cost all of one shilling. The partly demolished buildings on the right were part of Providence Place, also seen on page 34. This stood adjacent to Murray's bakery on Croft Terrace corner. Just beyond Providence Place can be seen the property at 8 South Street (illustrated on page 37), reckoned to be the oldest building in town and dating from c.1580. The man on the bike, Tuck Mather, a well-known local personality, is off to another spare time gardening job.

When it was presented to the town in 1904 this fountain was much appreciated by the horse-drawn traffic of the day, providing copious quantities of 'Adam's ale' to all who required it. On 22 November 1904, the day of its official opening, the proceedings were quickly abandoned when the horse-drawn fire brigade needed access to the Co-op's drapery department where a fire had broken out. Considerable damage was created by a combination of smoke and water. The superb granite fountain was presented to Egremont, his home town, by Alexander Cook, who had emigrated to America in 1854 and become an extremely successful industrialist. The fountain and attached trough were removed in 1922 when the site was chosen for the war memorial; they were relocated opposite the castle gates, where they can still be seen today.

Henry Lewthwaite (better known as Harry) was born in 1877. He was an adventurous youngster who saw the cycle as an exciting form of transport with far-reaching possibilities. Though the roads of his younger days were nothing like the smooth-surfaced ones we enjoy today, Harry looked ahead and realised that distances wouldn't seem so great if they could be traversed on two wheels instead of on foot. As an adolescent he obtained a bicycle and took it to pieces, learning about each part and its purpose before rebuilding it. He learned to ride with proficiency and his childhood dream of making a living out of cycles gradually became a reality. Commencing with repairs and sales from a shed in the garden, he went on to take over the Nos. 1 and 2 Main Street and in the course of time altered them into the double-fronted shop seen here. One side sold sweets and confectionery and the other cycles. In later years he moved to 24 Main Street, buying a plot of land which included a shop that had belonged to one of the town's tailors. By this time Harry had moved into a different type of transport – road haulage. He became sole contractor to the Whitehaven Brick & Tile Co., owning a small fleet of wagons which he housed in a large custom-built garage from where he worked for many years. Harry died aged 87 years, a great advocate of the old saying that hard worked never killed anyone.

Hunters Tea Stores were known far and wide before and after their arrival at Egremont, and were the town's first introduction to the world of the multiple-type grocer. Cleanliness was paramount in the working day of their staff, though their procedures would not have satisfied today's mania for hygiene. In 1906 the sight of delicious looking hams and sides of bacon lured customers into the store, where the smell was most tantalising. Cheeses of every kind and chests of tea from many countries scented the air, while the grinding of freshly roasted coffee beans made one long for a cup of the black stuff. Butter and lard were cut from huge blocks according to customers' needs, while sugar was weighed out in pounds, to be wrapped expertly by the assistants in strong blue paper before one's eyes. Dried fruits of kinds never seen before – juicy apricots, luscious figs, dark rich prunes, raisins, sultanas and currants – were all heaped in hessian sacks, each item contributing its own aroma to the store. It was a veritable Aladdin's cave of riches, all at unbelievable prices.

John Gainor was born in Whitehaven in 1863/64; his father, also named John, was a joiner. This remarkable picture shows the sort of display that John Gainor put on every market day at his shop at 9 Market Place (behind which he slaughtered his own meat). He had to compete with the farmer's wives who brought their goods to town, and also fight off fierce competition from out of town butchers who in even earlier days actually slaughtered animals on the street. At the time the word 'organic' had never been heard of, but every item he had for sale was organic in the true sense of he word. Cock chickens, geese, ducks, hares, rabbits, pork, mutton and beef were all killed on the premises. Freshness was the order of the day – there were no refrigerators then and meat needed to be sold quickly – a fast turnover was essential. John and his wife Isabella, pictured in the doorway, worked long and hard to establish their business in the early twentieth century. Isabella, mother to their six girls and two boys, died a young woman aged 35 years, after which a bereft John emigrated to Australia. One of their sons was killed as a member of the Australian Army in France during the First World War and is named as an Egremont casualty on the war memorial opposite their former home.

The release of a camera shutter, possibly as brief as $1/125$ of a second, has captured these hardy Thornhill pensioners in time. Ready to board one of Brownrigg's buses c.1950 for a tour of the eight lakes, they pose for a record of the occasion. This was a very popular tour of the time which Brownrigg's ran weekly throughout the summer season in the days when few ordinary workaday folk owned a car. Look closely and you might find Mam, Dad, Grandma or Granda in the picture.

This picture shows Egremont gasworks and office at Beck Green. Mary Jane Pickering lived at 7 Beck Green, along with her nephew Harold Bowman, who was aged 18 when this picture was taken in 1933. The gasworks were built by a small group of local businessmen who were far-sighted enough to see the benefits that a gas supply would bring to Egremont's residents – not to mention the profit they could derive from such an undertaking. As well as coal-gas, coke and tar were produced as by-products by the works.

These residents of Church Street are dressed in their best clothes, but the reason why is unclear. It can't have been just to have their photo taken or the other residents would have appeared too. A proud young man, hair nicely combed, stands beside his whippet accompanied by an equally proud sister. He's wearing a stiff collar and cravat and what looks very much like a sailor suit of the time. His clogs are polished, as are his sister's shoes. It must have been a Sunday.

A photograph of Egremont taken during a period of prosperity, when there was meat on the table and jam and butter on the bread. Miners with bait tins under their arms march resolutely to their workplace in the bowels of the earth, knowing they will receive a pay packet at the weekend. Such good times contrasted sharply with the days of depression when there was little work and the miners were forced to strike. During such periods of prosperity shopkeepers rejoiced, outstanding debts were paid, the river ran red and the pit hooters sounded their clarion calls summoning men to work. Youngsters lost their hungry looks and blossomed like the flowers of springtime. Trips to the sands at Seascale once more became the norm, hungry bellies were filled and new clothes purchased.